Me & You Journal

Fun, Prompted Journal to Get to Know Each Other Better

Catherine Adams

How to use this journal

Use the journal in the way that makes the most sense for you
and your partner. You can take turns writing your answers and
leaving where you left off with a bookmark.
You can read the questions out loud and answer and discuss
them.
If there are questions that don't apply or that either of you
don't like...skip them! Feel free to jump around or take
turns picking questions; they are in no specific order. There
is a blank page at the end of each question/section for more
writing space if needed and the blank pages at the end of the
journal can be used for you to come up with your own questions for each other.

I sincerely hope that you will be able to discuss your answers
with each other, bond, and above all else, have fun!

You woke up this morning with one of the following traits. Rank them from 1- 4 which you would want to be:

_1_ Stunningly Beautiful/Handsome

_2_ Crazy Smart

_4_ Super Popular

_3_ Wildly Talented

I think this is how my partner will rank their choices:

_1_ Stunningly Beautiful/Handsome

_4_ Crazy Smart

_2_ Super Popular

_3_ Wildly Talented

You woke up this morning with one of the following traits. Rank them from 1- 4 which you would want to be:

__1__ Stunningly Beautiful/Handsome

__2__ Crazy Smart

__4__ Super Popular

__3__ Wildly Talented

I think this is how my partner will rank their choices:

__1__ Stunningly Beautiful/Handsome

__4__ Crazy Smart

__2__ Super Popular

__3__ Wildly Talented

2

We answer/discuss

After you both have answered, discuss or write why you chose the traits you did or if you were surprised by each others choices:

_____

_____

_____

_____

_____

_____

_____

_____

_____

_____

_____

_____

_____

_____

_____

_____

_____

_____

_____

_____

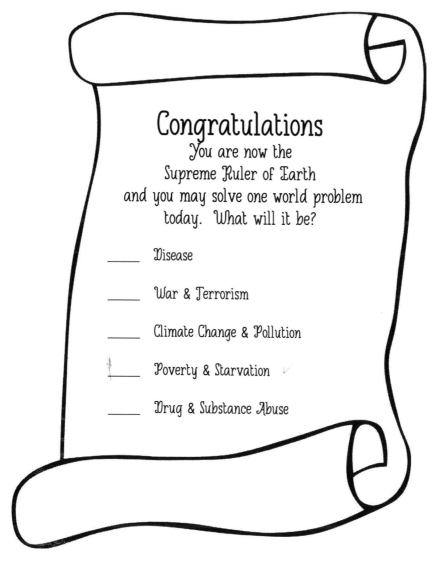

Congratulations
You are now the
Supreme Ruler of Earth
and you may solve one world problem
today. What will it be?

_____ Disease

_____ War & Terrorism

_____ Climate Change & Pollution

_____ Poverty & Starvation ✓

_____ Drug & Substance Abuse

Place a checkmark on the right to predict
your partners choice.

5

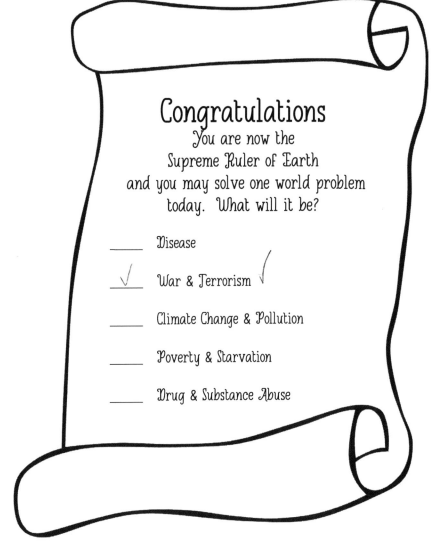

Congratulations

You are now the
Supreme Ruler of Earth
and you may solve one world problem
today. What will it be?

_____ Disease

√ War & Terrorism √

_____ Climate Change & Pollution

_____ Poverty & Starvation

_____ Drug & Substance Abuse

Place a checkmark on the right to predict
your partners choice.

6

We answer/discuss

After you both have answered, discuss or write why you made the choice you did or if you were surprised by each others choices. What would have been your second choices?

_____

_____

_____

_____

_____

_____

_____

_____

_____

_____

_____

_____

_____

_____

_____

_____

_____

_____

_____

When you were little where was the scariest place in your room?

_____   Under the bed

_____   In the closet

_____   Outside the window

_____   Somewhere else?

What did you think was hiding? What did you think would happen? (write/share/discuss)

_C_ _____

_____

_____

_____

_____

_____

_____

_____

9

When you were little where was the scariest place in your room?

_2_ Under the bed

_1_ In the closet

_3_ Outside the window

_4_ Somewhere else?

What did you think was hiding? What did you think would happen? (write/share/discuss)

_____
_____
_____
_____
_____
_____
_____
_____
_____

Did you tell anyone about your fears at the time?
Do you still fear something in your room (even though you know nothing's there)?
What do you think is the best way to help a child that is afraid of something in their room at night?

_____

_____

_____

_____

_____

_____

_____

_____

_____

_____

_____

_____

I answer

What 2 things in your life are you the most worried about right now?

Shayne

Saving for Retirement

What 2 things in your life are you the most worried about in the future?

_____

_____

Name one thing in your partners life that you think they are the most worried about right now:

Where to live

Who worries the most? (circle one)

(ME)   YOU

What 2 things in your life are you the most worried about right now?

Mom

Moms

What 2 things in your life are you the most worried about in the future?

Mom

Kids

Name one thing in your partners life that you think they are the most worried about right now:

R

Who worries the most? (circle one)

ME   YOU

Is there anything you can do about the things you're worried about? Is there anything you can do for each other?

_____

_____

_____

_____

_____

_____

_____

_____

_____

_____

_____

_____

_____

_____

_____

_____

_____

_____

_____

I answer

In high school do you think you were above or below average in the categories below? How do you think your partner will rate themselves?

I think I was:			You will say you were:	
Above	Below	In:	Above	Below
X		Science	'	
X		Sports		
X		English		
X		Popularity		
	X	Happiness		
	X	Trouble		
X		Shyness		
X		Working hard		

17

You answer

In high school do you think you were above or below average in the categories below? How do you think your partner will rate themselves?

I think I was:			You will say you were:	
Above	Below	In:	Above	Below
✓		Science	✓	
✓		Sports	✓	
✓		English	✓	
✓		Popularity	✓	
	✓	Happiness	✓	
✓		Trouble		✓
	✓	Shyness	✓	
✓		Working hard	✓	

18

We answer/discuss

Were you surprised by each other's choices?
What advice would you give someone just start-
ing high school? Is there a difference between
what you were then and what you are now?

_____

_____

_____

_____

_____

_____

_____

_____

_____

_____

_____

_____

_____

_____

_____

_____

_____ 19 _____

Do you believe in ghosts?
(yes / no

Why or why not?

_____
_____
_____
_____

Does your partner believe in ghosts?
yes/no

Do you believe in aliens?
yes / no

Why or why not?

_____
_____
_____
_____

Does your partner believe in aliens?
(yes/no

You answer

Do you believe in ghosts?
yes / no

Why or why not?

_MH_

_____

_____

_____

Does your partner believe in ghosts?
yes/no

◇◇◇◇◇◇◇◇◇◇◇◇◇◇◇◇◇◇◇◇◇◇◇◇◇◇

Do you believe in aliens?
yes / no

Why or why not?

_SP_

_____

_____

_____

Does your partner believe in aliens?
yes/no

Have you ever or do you know someone who has had a personal experience with either? Did you believe them? Which one do you hope exists more?

_____

_____

_____

_____

_____

_____

_____

_____

_____

_____

_____

_____

_____

_____

_____

_____

_____

_____

I answer

Family matters....

	Me	You
Who was more spoiled as a child?		X
When growing up whose family had more traditions?		X
Whose family has more crazy relatives?	X	
Who has/had the best grandparents?	X	
Who needs more approval from their family?		X
Who has the better relationship with their family?		X

Family matters....

	Me	You
Who was more spoiled as a child?	✓	
When growing up whose family had more traditions?	✓	
Whose family has more crazy relatives?		✓
Who has/had the best grandparents?		✓
Who needs more approval from their family?		✓
Who has the better relationship with their family?	✓	

Do you expect to take care of your parents when they are older? Do you expect your children to take care of you someday?

_____

_____

_____

_____

_____

_____

_____

_____

_____

_____

_____

_____

_____

_____

_____

_____

_____

_____

I answer

Who is...

	Me	You
sillier?		X
more of a nerd?		X
more likely to break a rule?		
more sensitive?	X	
more likely to give money to a ~~panhandler~~?		X
more logical?		X
more likely to talk their way out of a speeding ticket?		X
more honest?	depends	
more ambitious?		

You answer

Who is...

	Me	You
sillier?	✓	
more of a nerd?	✓	
more likely to break a rule?	✓	
more sensitive?		✓
more likely to give money to a panhandler?		✓
more logical?	✓	
more likely to talk their way out of a speeding ticket?	✓	
more honest?		✓
more ambitious?	✓	

Which attribute do you wish more described you?

_____
_____
_____
_____
_____
_____
_____
_____
_____
_____
_____
_____
_____
_____
_____
_____
_____

List 3 of your best traits:

_____

_____

_____

List 3 of your partners best traits:

_____

_____

_____

List 2 of your worst traits:

_____

_____

List 3 of your best traits:

_____

_____

_____

List 3 of your partners best traits:

_____

_____

_____

List 2 of your worst traits:

_____

_____

We answer/discuss

After you both have answered, discuss or write why you chose the traits you did or if you were surprised by each others choices:

_____

_____

_____

_____

_____

_____

_____

_____

_____

_____

_____

_____

_____

_____

_____

_____

_____

_____

I answer

List 2 fun things you think your partner should do more of:

_____

_____

List 2 fun things you should do more of:

_____

_____

List 2 fun things you should do more of together:

_____

_____

List one thing you've been putting off doing:

_____

List 2 fun things you think your partner should do more of:

_____

_____

List 2 fun things you should do more of:

_____

_____

List 2 fun things you should do more of together:

_____

_____

List one thing you've been putting off doing:

_____

What obstacles keep you from doing more fun things? Is there anything you could stop doing to give yourself more time to have fun?

_____
_____
_____
_____
_____
_____
_____
_____
_____
_____
_____
_____
_____
_____
_____
_____

I answer

Hola! Bonjour! Ciao!
Namaste! Salaam!
Ni Hau! Ola! Bula!

You woke up this morning fluent in a new language. What do you hope it is?

_____

Why?

_____

_____

_____

What would you want it to be for your partner?

_____

Why?

_____

_____

41

You answer

Hola! Bonjour! Ciao!
Namaste! Salaam!
Ni Hau! Ola! Bula!

You woke up this morning fluent in a new language. What do you hope it is?

_____

Why?

_____

_____

_____

What would you want it to be for your partner?

_____

Why?

_____

_____

What do you think would make the best common world language that everyone would learn as a child?

_____

_____

_____

_____

_____

_____

_____

_____

_____

_____

_____

_____

_____

_____

_____

List 3 things you are proud of yourself for this year:

_____

_____

_____

List 3 things you are proud of your partner for this year:

_____

_____

_____

45

List 3 things you are proud of yourself for this year:

_____

_____

_____

List 3 things you are proud of your partner for this year:

_____

_____

_____

Was is hard or easy to come up with these? What is one thing you wish you could add to your list?

_____

_____

_____

_____

_____

_____

_____

_____

_____

_____

_____

_____

_____

_____

_____

_____

_____

_____

In your ideal job/career what are the top three things that are most important for you?

_____ Great location

_____ Rewarding/love it

_____ Lots of travel

_____ High income

_____ Great co-workers

_____ Lots of time off

_____ Be my own boss

_____ Makes a difference

Place a check next to the two you think your partner will choose.

In your ideal job/career what are the top three things that are most important for you?

_____ Great location

_____ Rewarding/love it

_____ Lots of travel

_____ High income

_____ Great co-workers

_____ Lots of time off

_____ Be my own boss

_____ Makes a difference

Place a check next to the two you think your partner will choose.

Have you achieved the things you chose? Have they changed over time?

_____

_____

_____

_____

_____

_____

_____

_____

_____

_____

_____

_____

_____

_____

_____

_____

_____

51

What are 2 ways men have life easier than women?

_____

_____

What are 2 ways women have life easier than men?

_____

_____

If you could choose ahead of time the sex of your children, would you?

YES   NO

Would your partner?

YES   NO

What are 2 ways men have life easier than women?

_____

_____

What are 2 ways women have life easier than men?

_____

_____

If you could choose ahead of time the sex of your children, would you?

YES   NO

Would your partner?

YES   NO

We answer/discuss

What are ways life used to be easier for men and women than they are today? What are ways life used to be harder for men and women than they are today?

_____

_____

_____

_____

_____

_____

_____

_____

_____

_____

_____

_____

_____

_____

_____

_____

I answer

What do you think is better of the choices below?

	Winning $20	Finding $20	
	City	Country	
	Surprises	Planned events	
	Extra Credit	Curve	
	Running	Swimming	
	Spring	Fall	

What do you think your partner will choose?

	Winning $20	Finding $20	
	City	Country	
	Surprises	Planned events	
	Extra Credit	Curve	
	Running	Swimming	
	Spring	Fall	

What do you think is better of the think is better of the choices below?

Winning $20	Finding $20	
City	Country	
Surprises	Planned events	
Extra Credit	Curve	
Running	Swimming	
Spring	Fall	

What do you think your partner will choose?

Winning $20	Finding $20	
City	Country	
Surprises	Planned events	
Extra Credit	Curve	
Running	Swimming	
Spring	Fall	

If you found a suitcase full of money in the woods, what would you do? What if it contained $50, $500, or $50,000?

_____

_____

_____

_____

_____

_____

_____

_____

_____

_____

_____

_____

_____

_____

_____

_____

_____

_____

I answer

Circle the three life goals that you wish most for yourself. Place a check next to the ones you've done or are doing:

Being healthy

Having a successful career

Caring for others

Making the world a better place

Having a life partner

Being rich

Having children

Being happy

Having close friends

Being famous

Exploring/Traveling

61

Circle the three life goals that you wish most for yourself. Place a check next to the ones you've done or are doing:

Being healthy

Having a successful career

Caring for others

Making the world a better place

Having a life partner

Being rich

Having children

Being happy

Having close friends

Being famous

Exploring/Traveling

62

We answer/discuss

How have your priorities changed over time? What two things would be important to both of you in the future?

_____

_____

_____

_____

_____

_____

_____

_____

_____

_____

_____

_____

_____

_____

_____

_____

_____

_____

I answer

What 2 qualities do you think your partner needs most from you?

Encouragement	
Understanding and forgiveness	
A sense of humor	
Listening without giving advice	
Genuine interest in activities	
Open communication	
Unconditional love	
(add your own)	

Which 2 qualities do you need most from your partner?

Encouragement	
Understanding and forgiveness	
A sense of humor	
Listening without giving advice	
Genuine interest in activities	
Open communication	
Unconditional love	
(add your own)	

What 2 qualities do you think your partner needs most from you?

Encouragement	
Understanding and forgiveness	
A sense of humor	
Listening without giving advice	
Genuine interest in activities	
Open communication	
Unconditional love	
(add your own)	

Which 2 qualities do you need most from your partner?

Encouragement	
Understanding and forgiveness	
A sense of humor	
Listening without giving advice	
Genuine interest in activities	
Open communication	
Unconditional love	
(add your own)	

Discuss or write about one area that you could really use more support in from your partner:

_____

_____

_____

_____

_____

_____

_____

_____

_____

_____

_____

_____

_____

_____

_____

_____

_____

Do you believe in miracles?

YES / NO

Why or why not?

_____

_____

_____

_____

Does your partner believe in miracles?

YES / NO

Do you believe in guardian angels?

YES / NO

Why or why not?

_____

_____

_____

_____

Does your partner believe in guardian angels?

YES / NO

Do you believe in miracles?

YES / NO

Why or why not?

_____

_____

_____

_____

Does your partner believe in miracles?

YES / NO

Do you believe in guardian angels?

YES / NO

Why or why not?

_____

_____

_____

_____

Does your partner believe in guardian angels?

YES / NO

70

Have you ever or do you know someone who has had a personal experience with either? Did you believe them? Which one do you hope exists more?

_____

_____

_____

_____

_____

_____

_____

_____

_____

_____

_____

_____

_____

_____

_____

_____

I answer

The two of you are going off the grid and will live the next year in one of the following. Rank your top three choices and predict what your partner will choose:

	Me	You
an RV		
a yurt		
a tiny house		
a deluxe tree house		
a sailboat		
a tent		
a houseboat		
with friends and family		

The two of you are going off the grid and will live the next year in one of the following. Rank your top three choices and predict what your partner will choose:

	Me	You
an RV		
a yurt		
a tiny house		
a deluxe tree house		
a sailboat		
a tent		
a houseboat		
with friends and family		

Which one of you deals better with change? Is the idea of living in a different place exciting or stressful?

_____

_____

_____

_____

_____

_____

_____

_____

_____

_____

_____

_____

_____

_____

_____

_____

_____

I answer

Who worries more about:

	Me	You
the past		
the future		
money/finances		
what other people think		
being safe		
social issues		
what they eat		
world peace		
job security		
being/staying healthy		
family members		

Who worries more about:

	Me	You
the past		
the future		
money/finances		
what other people think		
being safe		
social issues		
what they eat		
world peace		
job security		
being/staying healthy		
family members		

Discuss what you think is a healthy amount of worry versus excessive worrying. What things help to reduce how much you worry?

_____

_____

_____

_____

_____

_____

_____

_____

_____

_____

_____

_____

_____

_____

_____

_____

_____

I answer

What are two things that you do well together?

_____

_____

What is one thing your partner makes look easy?

_____

_____

_____

What is one thing you are amazing at?

_____

_____

What are two things that you do well together?

_____

_____

What is one thing your partner makes look easy?

_____

_____

_____

What is one thing you are amazing at?

_____

_____

Do you work better together as a team or is it better if you divide and attack tasks separately? At work do you prefer working by yourself or in a group?

_____

_____

_____

_____

_____

_____

_____

_____

_____

_____

_____

_____

_____

_____

_____

_____

_____

What two things do you wish you could have more of this week?
What do you predict your partner will choose?

	Me	You
time		
money		
motivation		
love/affection		
happiness		
energy		
sleep		
peace/down-time		
fun/adventure		

What two things do you wish you could have more of this week?
What do you predict your partner will choose?

	Me	You
time		
money		
motivation		
love/affection		
happiness		
energy		
sleep		
peace/down-time		
fun/adventure		

We answer/discuss

Do you schedule time or plan for the choices you made? Is there a way you can help each other have more of what you wished for?

_____
_____
_____
_____
_____
_____
_____
_____
_____
_____
_____
_____
_____
_____
_____
_____
_____
_____

I answer

Which of you .... more?

	Me	You
dreams		
complains		
relaxes		
is in the bathroom		
finds happiness in little things		
judges other people		
gives advice		
communicates		
has fun		

You answer

Which of you .... more?

	Me	You
dreams		
complains		
relaxes		
is in the bathroom		
finds happiness in little things		
judges other people		
gives advice		
communicates		
has fun		

Did you agree? Which would be good for both of you to do more of? Less of?

_____

_____

_____

_____

_____

_____

_____

_____

_____

_____

_____

_____

_____

_____

_____

_____

_____

So...it turns out you get a super power on your next birthday that will last exactly one month. What do you hope it is?

_____ mind control

_____ invisibility

_____ super strength & speed

_____ ability to fly

_____ healing

How will you use it?

_____

_____

_____

What will your partner choose?

_____ mind control   _____ invisibility

_____ super strength & speed

_____ ability to fly   _____ healing

93

You answer

So...it turns out you get a super power on your next birthday that will last exactly one month. What do you hope it is?

_____ mind control

_____ invisibility

_____ super strength & speed

_____ ability to fly

_____ healing

How will you use it?

_____

_____

_____

What will your partner choose?

_____ mind control   _____ invisibility

_____ super strength & speed

_____ ability to fly   _____ healing

94

What if you got to keep the power, but it would shorten your life by 10 years. Would it be worth it? If everyone in the world had one of these powers what would be the best choice for all?

_____

_____

_____

_____

_____

_____

_____

_____

_____

_____

_____

_____

_____

_____

_____

_____

_____

_____

I answer

Do you believe in karma?
yes / no

Why or why not?

_____

_____

_____

_____

Does your partner believe in karma?
yes/no

◇◇◇◇◇◇◇◇◇◇◇◇◇◇◇◇◇◇◇◇◇◇◇◇◇◇

Do you believe in love at first sight?
yes / no

Why or why not?

_____

_____

_____

_____

Does your partner believe in love at first sight?
yes/no

97

Do you believe in karma?
yes / no

Why or why not?

_____

_____

_____

_____

Does your partner believe in karma?
yes/no

◇◇

Do you believe in love at first sight?
yes / no

Why or why not?

_____

_____

_____

_____

Does your partner believe in love at first
sight?
yes/no

98

Have you ever or do you know someone who has had a personal experience with either? Did you believe them? Which one do you hope exists more?

_____

_____

_____

_____

_____

_____

_____

_____

_____

_____

_____

_____

_____

_____

_____

_____

_____

You just won a time travel trip!

Do you want to go:

_____   to the past

_____   to the future

what period of time in the past or how far into the future?

_____

_____

What would you want to see or do?

_____

_____

Do you think your partner will want to go:

_____   to the past

_____   to the future

You just won a time travel trip!

Do you want to go:

_____ to the past

_____ to the future

what period of time in the past or how far into the future?

_____

_____

What would you want to see or do?

_____

_____

Do you think your partner will want to go:

_____ to the past

_____ to the future

We answer/discuss

Who would you want to meet? Where would you like to go together? If you had to be there permanently, would you make the same choice?

_____

_____

_____

_____

_____

_____

_____

_____

_____

_____

_____

_____

_____

_____

_____

_____

I answer

You just won a **Vacation Home** that you can use every weekend. The perfect place would be...(check one in each group)

located

_____ on the oceanfront

_____ in the mountains

_____ by a lake

with a great view of the

_____ sunrise

_____ sunset

There would be plenty of

_____ outdoor activities

_____ indoor activities

and lots of

_____ quiet time

_____ parties

105

You just won a **Vacation Home** that you can use every weekend. The perfect place would be...(check one in each group)

located

_____ on the oceanfront

_____ in the mountains

_____ by a lake

with a great view of the

_____ sunrise

_____ sunset

There would be plenty of

_____ outdoor activities

_____ indoor activities

and lots of

_____ quiet time

_____ parties

106

If you won a vacation home together, where would you hope it would be? At the beach, in the mountains, on a lake? In this country or a different country?

_____

_____

_____

_____

_____

_____

_____

_____

_____

_____

_____

_____

_____

_____

_____

_____

_____

I answer

Do you agree or disagree with the following?

	agree	dis-agree
Everyone has a soulmate.		
The death penalty should be eliminated.		
Military service should be mandatory.		
Social media is a waste of time.		
Marriage is outdated.		
Nice guys finish last.		
Marijuana should be legalized nationally.		
Countries should have open borders.		
Always tell the truth.		
The drinking age should be lowered.		

Do you agree or disagree with the following?

	agree	dis-agree
Everyone has a soulmate.		
The death penalty should be eliminated.		
Military service should be mandatory.		
Social media is a waste of time.		
Marriage is outdated.		
Nice guys finish last.		
Marijuana should be legalized nationally.		
Countries should have open borders.		
Always tell the truth.		
The drinking age should be lowered.		

We answer/discuss

After you both have answered, discuss or write if you were surprised by each others choices:

_____

_____

_____

_____

_____

_____

_____

_____

_____

_____

_____

_____

_____

_____

_____

_____

_____

_____

I answer

Question:

_____

_____

_____

Answer:

_____

_____

_____

_____

_____

_____

_____

_____

_____

_____

_____

_____

_____

_____

_____

_____

Question:

_____

_____

_____

Answer:

_____

_____

_____

_____

_____

_____

_____

_____

_____

_____

_____

_____

_____

_____

_____

113

I answer

Question:

_____

_____

_____

Answer:

_____

_____

_____

_____

_____

_____

_____

_____

_____

_____

_____

_____

_____

_____

_____

_____

_____

You answer

Question:

_____

_____

_____

Answer:

_____

_____

_____

_____

_____

_____

_____

_____

_____

_____

_____

_____

_____

_____

_____

_____

I answer

Question:

_____

_____

_____

Answer:

_____

_____

_____

_____

_____

_____

_____

_____

_____

_____

_____

_____

_____

_____

_____

_____

_____

You answer

Question:

_____

_____

_____

Answer:

_____

_____

_____

_____

_____

_____

_____

_____

_____

_____

_____

_____

_____

_____

_____

_____

I answer

Question:

_____

_____

_____

Answer:

_____

_____

_____

_____

_____

_____

_____

_____

_____

_____

_____

_____

_____

_____

_____

_____

_____

_____

You answer

Question:

_____

_____

_____

Answer:

_____

_____

_____

_____

_____

_____

_____

_____

_____

_____

_____

_____

_____

_____

_____

I answer

Question:
_____
_____
_____

Answer:
_____
_____
_____
_____
_____
_____
_____
_____
_____
_____
_____
_____
_____
_____
_____
_____
_____

You answer

Question:

_____

_____

_____

Answer:

_____

_____

_____

_____

_____

_____

_____

_____

_____

_____

_____

_____

_____

_____

_____

_____

I answer

Question:

_____

_____

_____

Answer:

_____

_____

_____

_____

_____

_____

_____

_____

_____

_____

_____

_____

_____

_____

_____

_____

You answer

Question:

_____

_____

_____

Answer:

_____

_____

_____

_____

_____

_____

_____

_____

_____

_____

_____

_____

_____

_____

_____

_____

_____

I answer

Question:

_____

_____

_____

Answer:

_____

_____

_____

_____

_____

_____

_____

_____

_____

_____

_____

_____

_____

_____

_____

_____

You answer

Question:

_____

_____

_____

Answer:

_____

_____

_____

_____

_____

_____

_____

_____

_____

_____

_____

_____

_____

_____

_____

_____

47532448R00074

Made in the USA
Columbia, SC
02 January 2019